# RICHARD SCARRY

## ABC
## Word Book

# Aa Bb Cc

# Gg Hh Ii

# Mm Nn Oo

# Ss Tt Uu

# Xx Yy

# Dd Ee Ff

# Jj Kk Ll

# Pp Qq Rr

# Vv Ww

# Zz

jet plane

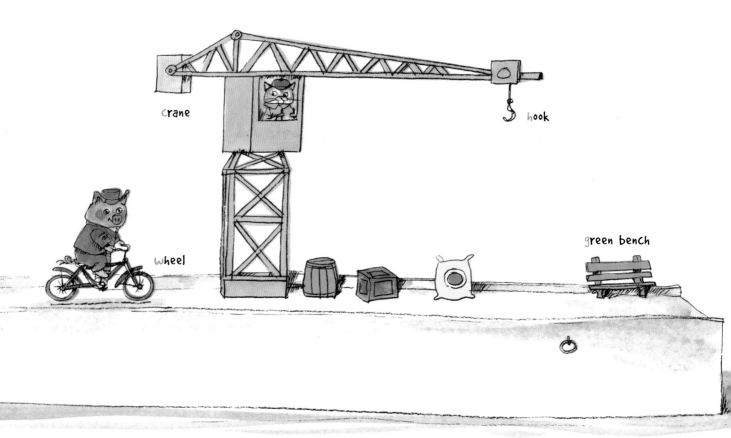

crane

hook

wheel

green bench

First published in Great Britain in 1971
This edition published by HarperCollins Children's Books in 2006
HarperCollins Children's Books is a division of HarperCollins Publishers Ltd.

1 3 5 7 9 10 8 6 4 2
0-00-718927-3

© 1971 Richard Scarry Corporation

Printed and bound in China

# RICHARD SCARRY

# ABC
# Word Book

bridge

BARBER

car

fisherman

mouse

yacht

submarine

HarperCollins *Children's Books*

# Aa

As Mother Cat was driving Father Cat to the airport, she had an accident.

vintage car

policeman

crane

repair van on the way to the accident

ambulance

hydrant

taxi

attendant

arm

umbrella

PETROL STATION

cane

hat

farmer

hay cart

a racing car going fast

MAIL
AIR MAIL

REFUSE REMOVAL

The dustbin man has a flat tyre.
He is sad.

jack

flat tyre

DANGER

sack of potatoes

bag of asparagus

traffic signal

basket of apples

manhole

farm truck

ABC FARM

CRASH!

car

PARKING

baby pram

No one was hurt in the accident because
everybody was wearing a seatbelt.

pavement

# Aa

airliner

tail

wind vane

stewardess

hangar

boarding stairs

tramp

father cat

FOLLOW ME

a flat rabbit

At the airport a plane is about to land all alone. The aviator is landing by parachute.

Hilda running out of the way to safety

parachute

flag

a hot air balloon

anchor

SWISSAIR

radar nose

fuel tank

landing gear

a bear asleep
in the shade

FUEL

fuel-tank lorry

luggage wagon train

bag          bag          bag

A gang of ants rushing away, fast!

pad

easel

palette

Watch out! Mother Cat!
Step on the accelerator!

water jar          artist          paint brush

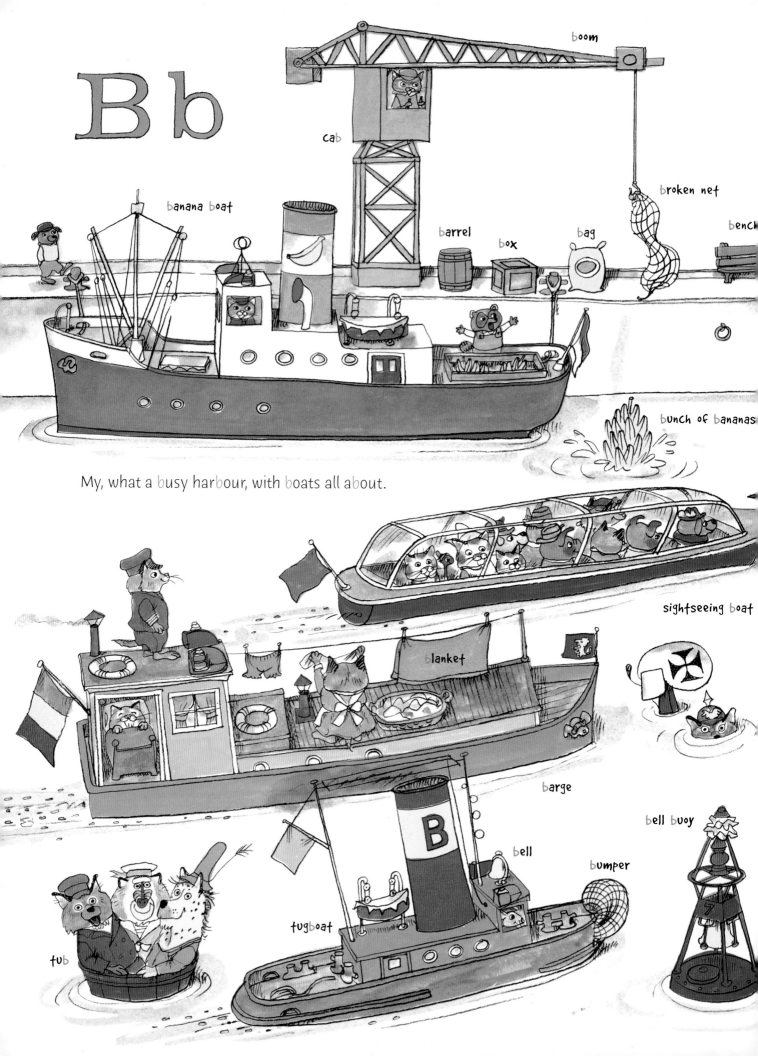

# B b

boom

cab

banana boat

barrel

box

bag

broken net

bench

bunch of bananas

My, what a busy harbour, with boats all about.

sightseeing boat

blanket

barge

bell buoy

bell

bumper

tugboat

tub

a raised bridge

a brick building

ing-boat

bicycle

boy

BARBER

BAKERY

bobber

Captain Salty waves from the bridge
of his big, blue ship.

submarine

tuba

radio cabin

book

ow

brush

blouse

boot

broom

boat bottom

bottle

# C c

A crowd came to Tiger Cat's picnic.
Everyone licked ice cream cones and
danced to the lively music.

ice cream cone

cup

A couple of mice served cider
from a cement mixer.

Tiger Cat cooked popcorn.
The cover wasn't closed.
Crackle! Crackle! Pop!
Be careful, Tiger Cat!

a cook's cap

POP
CORN

packet

cover

can

coffeepot

can opener

camp stove

Rudolf cracked up.

cornet

camera

Crab caught popcorn in his claws.

accordion

Lowly danced in a circle with a piece of celery.

candle

Clarence couldn't count the biscuits he ate.

Curly Pig accidentally fell into the centre of the cake. CRASH!

What a crazy, cuckoo picnic!

# Ch ch

It's a chilly day, but everyone is full of good cheer. Christmas is tomorrow. The bells chime in the church steeple.

church

a chimney sweep
scratching his itchy chin

CHOICE
and
CHEAP
MEAT
CHARLES CHIMP

The yule log is attached to the sled with a chain.

butcher

latch

chickens

chimney

children carolling

kerchief

patch

Ma Pig is chatting with Mrs. Chipmunk. She is also burning the chop for her children's lunch. She is a champion chatterbox.

China

chair

stitch

bench

match

wristwatch

# D d

The dizzy, daffy, dopey bulldozer driver!
What does he think he is doing? He is dangerous.
He has knocked down the building, and the
chemist is good and mad.

a standing
road grader

a damaged
drum

a muddy lady

mud puddle

indigo hat

a dusty doctor

dust

bull dozer

medicine bag

Wild Bill Hiccup

DETOUR

a dumped-over dumping lorry

derrick

board

drill

a scared ditch digger

Where is
Huckle hiding?

ladder

a deep ditch

DANGER

door

a dozen doughnuts

DOUGHNUTS

delivery man

# E e

Ernie Elephant and his excellent firemen have just driven up to extinguish an enormous fire. Mother Rabbit is screaming for help. Do not fear! They will save her.

helmet

bee

siren

bell

pumper engine

extra hose

a fireman eating blackberry pie

reel

mouse

eye

hen

empty basket

eggs

red fire engine

broken egg

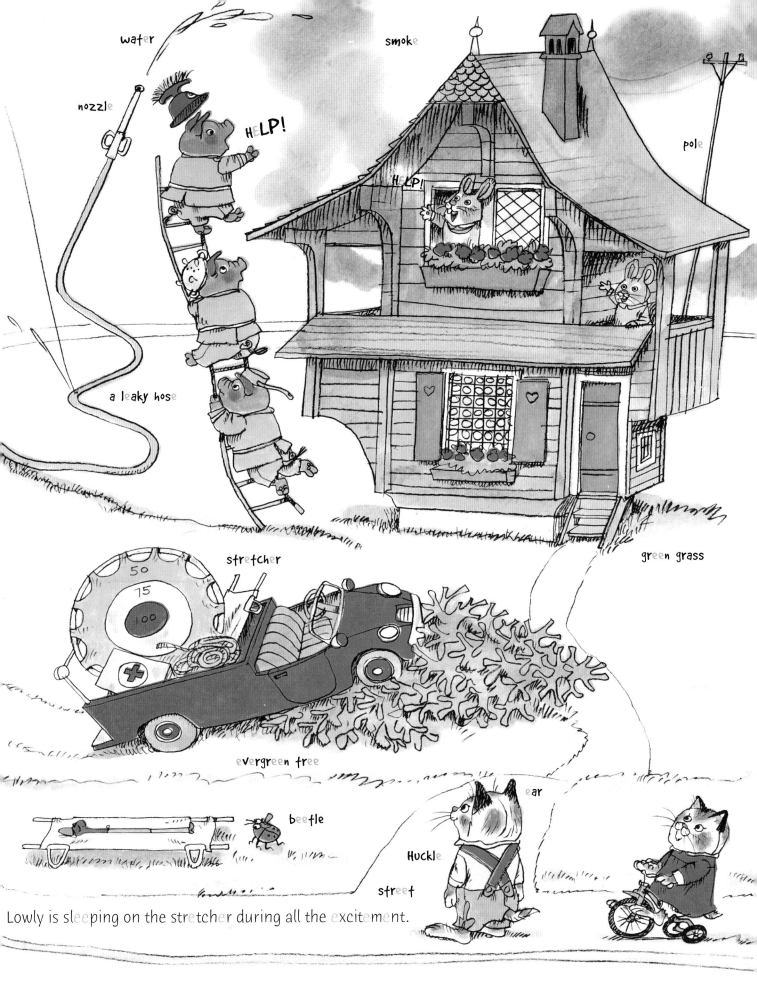

water

smoke

nozzle

HELP!

HELP!

pole

a leaky hose

stretcher

green grass

50
75
100

evergreen tree

ear

beetle

Huckle

street

Lowly is sleeping on the stretcher during all the excitement.

Look at the three firemen on a leaning ladder. Are they going to topple over?

# F f

a fast freight train

giraffe

leaf

a fruit tree

fence

fertilizer

field

pitchfor

Farmer Fox grows food in the fields for his family. There are five furry foxes hiding in the farmhouse. Can you find them?

front wheels

three frankfurters

a funny face

pole

flag

farmhouse roof

forest

flower

flow

fireplace

flames

file

muffins

flour

floor

a fat fish

one fly

Five flies follow
each other in a
single file.

Wolf and his friend
Freddy Frog.

Huckle fell flat on his face.

foot

four fish

knife

a floating cap

# G g

GREASY GEORGE'S
GORGEOUS GARAGE

What is going on at Greasy George's garage?

a great big green lorry

GOOD PETROL

girl

green pump

GOOD PETROL

hot dog

bag

grill

a guitar strin[g]

Goofy Goose is going to take a group of gabby goslings to the picnic grounds. Ugh! He is groaning at the thought.

GO RIGHT

a midget car

a gardener by a glass greenhouse

The telephone is ringing. B-r-r-i-n-g-g!

a vegetable garden

engine

Grandma is grinning and giggling.

BARGAIN SALE

glasses

globs of grease

bang!
clang!

Greasy George is greasing a car with his grease gun. He is wearing gloves.

detergent

glue

sponge

Something is wrong here but the mechanic is fixing it.

Huckle is wearing racing goggles.

CAR WASH INSIDE AND OUTSIDE

# H h

Here is a happy home. However, someone is unhappy.
Father hired a helper to fix the roof shingles and the helper
hit his thumb with the hammer. "OUCH!" he howled.

a head poking through a hole in a hat

heart

shutter

children

hatchet

hoe

Ha-ha!

hose

Huckle has a very high hat on his
head and a horn in his hands.
He is blowing hard.

a hard rock

a helicopter hovering high above the earth

a tree house

branch

Someone is hiding in a heap of clothes.

hook

hanger

hot water

shower

Hurry, Mother! Something is happening to the spaghetti.

honey    pitcher

dish

ketchup

a hen in a hurry

bush

Father is digging a hole in which to plant a bush.

shovel

hole

wheelbarrow

# I i

It is a very windy day. The sails of the windmill were spinning around fast until Uncle Irving's kite string tied them up. The Miller is furious. He has an important order to fill.

Rudolf's diving high-flyer lost its wings in flight. Rudolf is going swimming with his friends.

pillow

pipe

a high hill

Willy, a little imp, is licking an ice cream cone and spilling it in Uncle Irving's shirt.

wire fence

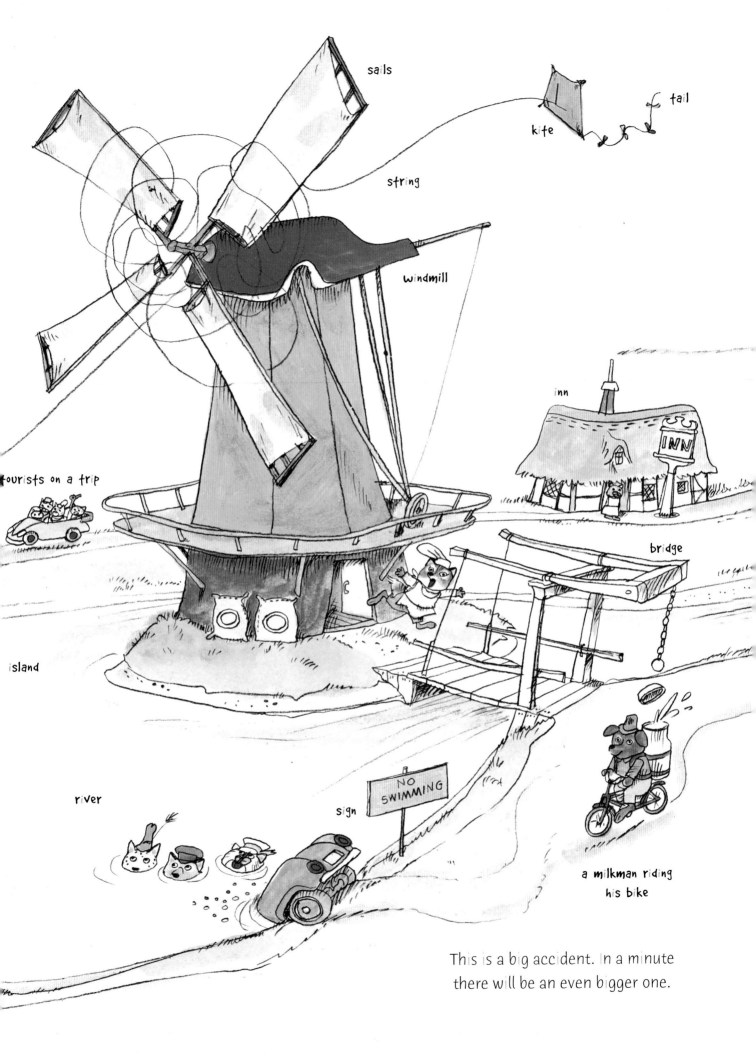

sails

kite

tail

string

windmill

inn

tourists on a trip

bridge

island

river

sign

NO SWIMMING

a milkman riding his bike

This is a big accident. In a minute there will be an even bigger one.

# J j

jungle gym

Hilda just jammed a grapefruit between her
jaws and went c-r-u-n-c-h. Was it juicy, Hilda?

jaw

jewel

jug

pyjamas

jumping Jill

jumbo-sized lantern

a jet pilot on a joy ride

parachute jumper

Janitor Joe enjoys driving his jeep.

This juggler is juggling jars of jam.

jacket

A joyful jester is playing jolly jingles on his banjo.

# K k

The King is having a snack. He is licking a gherkin. Kangaroo is skating in with a cake she has baked for the King. Would you like to share his snack?

a turkey soaking in the sink

king

Duck likes to drink milk.

gherkin

fork

a basket of crackers

napkin

baked bricks

key

knife

pocket

broken leg

sock

Kitten is sucking milk through a straw.

The cuckoo clock goes tick-tock.

back door

keyhole

a mouse peeking through a crack

ketchup

kettle

cook

stirring stick

book

a thick steak

a leaky bucket

cake

kangaroo

a kiss

smack!

skate

pumpkin

truck

Huckle has a pumpkin in the back of his truck.

# L l

A large steamroller is rolling wildly over the land.
Look out, all you people, or you will be flattened!

signal light

a leaning sign

a flat limousine

The postman slipped
and lost a lot of letters.

a flat bicycle

a flat lawn mower

a leaning laundry pole

a little girl licking a lollipop

Mrs. Pig is losing her clean laundry. She calls
out loudly, "let go of my laundry! And please
leave my lovely flowers alone."

oil barrel

leap frog

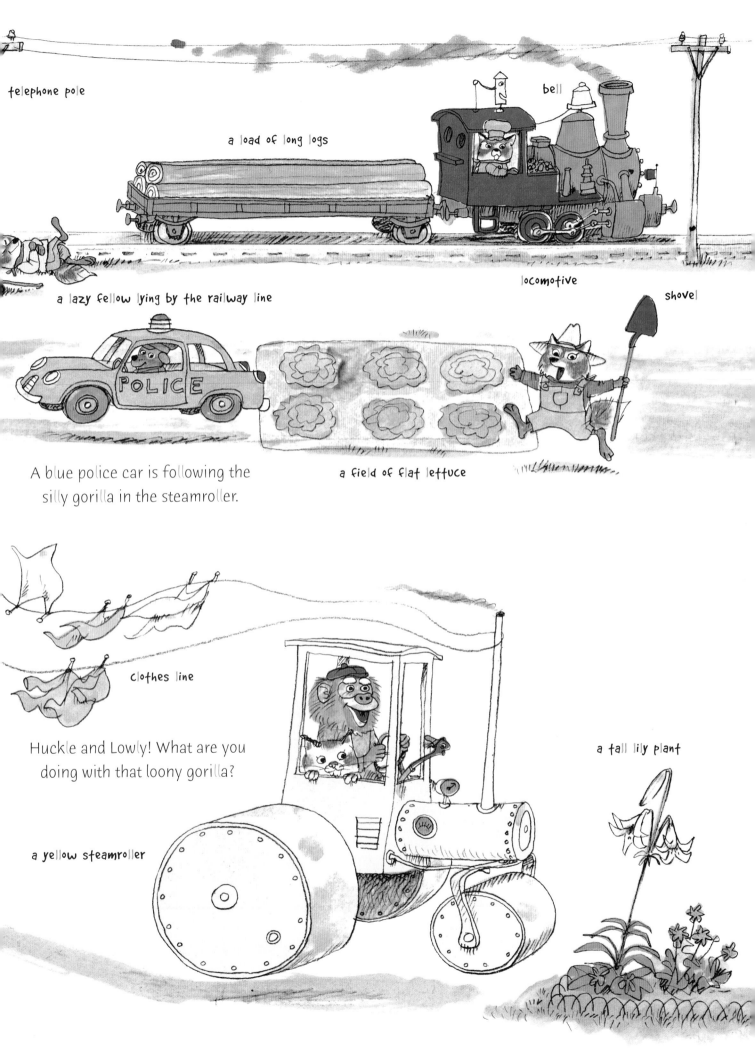

telephone pole

a load of long logs

bell

locomotive

shovel

a lazy fellow lying by the railway line

POLICE

a field of flat lettuce

A blue police car is following the
silly gorilla in the steamroller.

clothes line

Huckle and Lowly! What are you
doing with that loony gorilla?

a tall lily plant

a yellow steamroller

# Mm

mouse

midget car

drum

trombone

merry firemen making music

cement mixer

ambulance

medicine

medical instruments

ice cream man

bump!

Doctor Monday on a bumpy road

mail van

milk bottles

milk lorry

bumper

mirror

monkey wrench

monument

mop

motorcycle

WILLIAM TELL

PLUMBER

smoke

plumber's van

MAIL

MILK

M101

Something is the matter with Mummy's motor. A mechanic is trying to make it go. Father Pig is stuck in the messy, muddy road. How mad he is! Oh, my!

a messy, muddy road

SPEED LIMIT 60 M.P.H.

# N n

aeroplane

orange crane

nose

Rudolf's plane landed in a pond.
A crane yanked it out.

a broken fence

net

a bunch of bananas

a policeman running

HIGH STREET

sign

another runner
in pink trousers

a nice nursemaid and
an infant napping

nine pine trees in a long lor

pennant

balloon

a shining sun

anchor

Another aeroplane landed in the pond
– and then another. No more, please.
That is certainly enough!

bench

newspaper

NEWS STAND

a new tie

a painter painting lines

Uncle Ned

a convertible on a saloon
on a station wagon

TREE
NURSERY

hydrant

NO PARKING

# Oo

Oh, my! See how many people have come down to the harbour to see the boats dock.

bow
boy
lookout
motorboat
dock
horn
toot!
captain fox
pilot house
boat
bow
bu
portholes
door
Sailor Dog overboard!
rose
octopus
hello!
goodbye!
rowing-boat
oar
top
bottle
bottom
Codfish in oil skins
boots
sole

GOOD FOOD SHOP

trolley bus

road

Lowly Worm

an old goat looking
out of a window

a young goat
not looking
where he
is going

O.K.
HOTEL

owl tossing
a rope

bow

arrow

pole

soldier in armour

tower

Someone forgot to stop. The boat is going
down to the bottom of the harbour.

clock

shore

wagon

cannon

ogre in dungeon

old fort

# P p

Pretty Polly Pig is having a party. She is playing the piano. Plink! Plink! All the people are happy.

palm

trumpet

piano

plump pig

pin

pot

platform

piper

Porcupine goes
poo-poo-pa-doo
on his saxophone.

bagpipe

saxophone player

sharp poin

plaid

piccolo

spectacles

parrot

penguin

pelican eating
peanuts

puffin

present

a person peeling apples
up in a lamp

peach

pineapple

pear

Peter is pushing Paul.
Stop that, Peter.
Don't be a pest!

plate

a group of pigs

carpet

Huckle slips and drops
the plum pudding. Lowly jumps
up and catches it. Put it back
on the plate, Lowly!

Little Sister pours pink punch
from a pint jug into a paper cup.
Don't spill, please.

plop!

pie

punch bowl

teapot

# Q q

The Queen is playing croquet with her friends.
They seem to be quarrelling. Please! Let's be quiet!

The Queen in her quilted robe.

Two squirrels are playing quoits.

quit it!

Quincy squeezes his water gun and water squirts out.

It hits a squid in his aquarium.

Quite a nice shot, Queenie!

Two girls play hopscotch on numbered squares.

mosquito

a quart of milk

7 8
6
4 5
3
2
1

# R r

G-r-r-r!

rabbit ear

rudder

rowing-boat

pirate

raft

The Rapid Rabbits were racing the river Rascals in a rowing-boat race up the river. The steerer steered right onto a rock. C-r-u-n-c-h! The race was over. He was in a furious rage.

drowning Lowly Worm

life ring

Huckle rescuing a swimmer

umbrella

Rhinoceros is rather peculiar. He prefers not to get wet when he goes into the water.

Bravo!

raincoat

reeds

a hungry beggar wearing rags

rubber boots

ribbon

radio

a tired rower
resting

carrot

rock

the losers

the winners

A rooster can crow. Can a crow rooster?

outboard motor

rope

water ski

raccoon

THREE STAR
RESTAURANT

terrace

very bad manners

REST
ROOM
→

A waiter is carrying a tray of fruit to a customer.
Who left that chair where someone would surely trip over it?

# S s

brush

smack!

stilts

scout

scooter

Daddy Pig came into the house and kissed Mummy.
"What's for supper?" he asked.
"Your seven silly cousins are visiting us for several days," answered Mummy.
"They wish to cook and serve our meals to us. They are making a super surprise supper now."
"Something does smell delicious," said Daddy. "Let's see what it is that smells so good."
Oh! Such a sight they saw!

Sam was washing dishes in the sink.

Silas was searching for some stockings in the storage barrel.

sock

switch

saucer

soup bowl

spoon

glass

sieve

sink

smash!

steam

Sandy was adding soap and sticky syrup to the stew.

sauce

stick

SOAP

Sidney was slowly stirring the stew.

Stanley was spilling a strainer of slippery spaghetti.

sack

Simon was pouring sweet strawberries into the simmering soup.

sausages

sailing-boat

Sylvester was slicing and tossing salami.

scissors

sugar

salt

I hope everyone's stomach will be satisfied with this super surprise supper!

sandwich

# Sh sh

shade

shaving brush

shell

shelf

sharp shears

a shoulder shawl

wash tub

shoe

What a shame! Mother Bear washed a shirt and it shrank.
Father Bear is blushing with embarrassment.

washing-line

a sheet with shapes shaking inside it

shampoo

splish!

splash!

splosh!

shower

a shaggy mop

mashed potatoes

A sheep in shabby clothes crashed through the door to
show what his brushes could do. One could even turn on the shower!
Mother told him to shut the door. The cold air was making her shiver.

Children were dashing and rushing
about, shrieking and shouting, pushing
and shoving. Hush, children, be silent!
I mean, hush, children, be silent!

# T t

Take a look at the terrible accident. A train has hit a truck that contained ten thousand tomatoes. What a sight!

signal tower

conductor

tickets

tracks

terrified travellers on a train trip

kite

treetop

tennis racket

net

rabbit

tennis court

string

a turtle in a tub of hot bath water

towel

tree trunk

stump

a toad tootling on a toadstool

tow truck

trumpet

smokestack

tomatoes

tyres

tennis ball

a crossing gate torn in two

truck

tent

pot

street

tyre tracks

television set

lantern

stone

table

tepee

Little Sister riding her tricycle

tractor

rut

Rudolf returned to earth too fast and left a great rut
in the dirt. Look! You're on television, Rudolf!

# Th th

King Theodore Thaddeus walked down the path without thinking wither he was going. He walked into a thicket of thistles.

thistles

Thrashing about, he found he was stuck to them. This, he thought, is a terrible thing! Then he threw off his thick cloth suit and in three seconds he was free.

However, the weather was cold, and all he had on were thin underthings. It is not healthy to wear nothing but that in the cold.

scythe

Just then Thelma, a nice lady, came along.
"WHAT ON EARTH!" she said. "Something must
be done."

She cut some straw with her scythe. Then
she put a thimble on her thumb, and with
her needle and thread she made Theodore
Thaddeus a new suit of straw thatch. King
Theodore Thaddeus thanked Thelma a
thousand times.

They went back to his castle together, and sat within before the hearth. Then King
Theodore Thaddeus thought…Why not?
Right then and there he asked Thelma to be his queen and share his throne with
him. Thelma was breathless. Nevertheless… she said "YES!"
What do you think of that?!

hearth

When rain pours down, the ground turns to mud. Uncle Louie's car has sunk under the surface. Tough luck, Louie!

house

The sound of music is coming from upstairs.

Huckle playing a flute

Lowly playing a huge tuba

Crunch! Munch!
Hilda is eating her lunch outside the house.
Down below, a bulldozer is stuck in the muck.

Paul is pulling and grunting. Ugh!

You, there! Hurry up and shut the door before the house is full of mud.

Paddy is pushing.

underwear

Even Rudolf has put up his umbrella.
Too bad he is upside down.

BUTCHER

Aunt Ursula is jumping home after
buying enough sausages for supper.

Duck is busy unloading nuts
out of his dump truck.

nuts

FOURTH AVENUE

a muddy uniform

Sergeant Murphy is shouting loudly, "Don't clutter up the avenue!"

# V v

aviator

weather vane

glove

A vintage car is driving through a village and over a very high viaduct. This roving family is going to visit relatives.

VILLAGE OF LOVE

two chatting wives

viaduct

a van with five jugs of vinegar

a violent driver

river

a brave cat diving to save a mouse

violets

volcano

grape vines

Vincent lives in a cave. He is shaving his lovely face.

a jolly violin player

Victor, the Viking, is arriving home in his sailing vessel after a very long voyage.

# W w

The weather is wild and windy.
The whole town is blowing away.

wig

walrus

a window washer
wiping a window

woods

Lowly Worm inside a watermelon

water

a waiter losing his warm stew

wait!

paw

wrist watch

Wolf howling at his hat

Huckle wearing a weight to hold him down

a whirring, twirling windmill

a wet towel

a wool sweater

owl growing wheat in a meadow

wrench

a girl watching at the window

a witch in a wheelbarrow

a new wooden wagon

wheel

two fowl squawking

two wiggling wrestlers

a walnut on a wall

# X x

axe

A fox and an ox are mixing alphabet soup in a box.
It is excellent exercise.

exhaust

There are exactly six saxophone
players in the taxi.

# Y y

Yak is playing with his yo-yo.

Why is the little pig crying? He has his own toy.

yacht

# Z z

z-z-z-o-o-m!

a hat that is the wrong size

bulldozer

blazer

a zebra in a zipper jacket

Lowly is snoozing.

chimpanzee

exit    nix

razzle dazzle    yoo hoo

tin lizzie

a dozing baby

buzzer

Yellow stripes show the safety zone.

Izzy lizard is dizzy. He is walking a zigzag.